Copyright © 2026 Durell Fisher
All rights reserved.

No part of this book may be reproduced or transmitted in any form or by any means without written permission from the author,

except for brief quotation in review.

ISBN: 979-8-218-91827-9

First edition 2026.

Author's Declaration of Faith

I am a Christian, and I wholeheartedly believe in Christianity. This book is not written to discredit faith, but to present facts from my life experiences, research, and study. It examines the systems and traditions that have shaped leadership paths differently for Black men and White men. My conviction in Christ is still the foundation of my life, and my critique is aimed at institutions and historical forces, not at the gospel of Jesus Christ.

Author's Background Note

Durell J. Fisher was raised in a household rooted in Christian faith. His mother and his sister are both Baptist ministers, and their prayers, teaching, and example helped shape his spiritual foundation.

Although his journey included seasons of struggle, questioning, and change, his life has always been surrounded by the influence of the church, the Word of God, and women of faith who believed in his calling long before he understood it.

Dedication

To the people who raised me, prayed for me, and challenged me to see beyond the Church – this is for you.

Acknowledgement

Special thank you to my wife, Tomiko Fisher, for supporting m through this journey.

Introduction

What constrained me to write this book is deeply rooted in the condition of Black people in North America. In many neighborhoods, there's a church on every corner, yet families are wrestling with the same old enemies: poverty, underfunded schools, violence, and the quiet despair that comes with being told to wait. I'm fifty-five. From the time I left my mother's womb, I saw churches and heard sermons. As a young man, I chose the streets instead – thinking power lived there. Later, I learned that path led nowhere.

I'm now an ordained deacon. I love the church. I love the Word. But I cannot pretend that every word preached is rooted in power that sets captives free. This book asks a hard question: Why do so many Black men ascend to the pulpit while White men pursue and occupy the visible seats of national and global leadership? What have history and habit taught us about where to see authority? And how do we transform spiritual authority to material justice?

On the plantation, faith kept families alive. Mothers prayed, fathers endured, and children learned how to survive. The church became a haven and an organizing center – sometimes a shelter, sometimes a stage. That legacy runs deep. For generations, the pulpit was the first and most accessible "office" a Black man could hold with dignity. Yet the pulpit becomes the only office – if sermons replace strategies and comfort replaces confrontation – then the same institution that preserved us can also limit us.

This book is not an attack on belief. It is a demand that belief does work – that it feels the hungry, builds businesses, shapes policy, and produces leaders who can navigate city hall and the World bank, school boards, and the U.N. I draw on voices that wrestled with these tensions – Malcolm X, Elijah Muhammad, Louis Farrakhan, Julia Hare, Nathan Hare, and even comments by Alec Baldwin about America's narrow global lens. Their perspectives are not identical; sometimes they clash. But together they challenge us to move beyond symbolic power and into the hard craft of liberation.

If faith without works is dead, then preaching without power is just noise. The chapters ahead trace how we got here, what keeps us here, and what it takes to leave the pulpit's walls for the world's tables – without losing our soul.

Table of Contents

Chapter 1 – Plantation Faith & the Making of the Pulpit 1

Chapter 2 – The Preacher as the First "Office" for Black Men: A Platform When Few Existed 3

Chapter 3 – Money, Malachi, and Misreadings: The Sacred Text Meets the Ledger................ 7

Chapter 4 – Prosperity vs. Prophecy - Introduction: The Cross or the Cadillac? 11

Chapter 5 – The Politics of Preaching - Introduction: From Sermon to Strategy 15

Chapter 6 – Black Church vs. White Church - Introduction: Two Sanctuaries, Two Stories 19

Chapter 7 – Power, Psychology, and Control - Introduction: The Battle for the Mind 23

Chapter 8 – A Legacy of Resistance Introduction: Prophets or Puppets? 27

Chapter 9 – The Global Stage - Introduction: From Pulpit to Presidency 30

Chapter 10 – The Future of Black Leadership - Introduction: Beyond the Walls 33

Chapter 11 – A Call to Action - Introduction: From Question to Charge 36

Chapter 12 – The Difference Between a White Man's Theology Training vs. a Black Man's Training - Introduction: Same Scriptures, Different Schools 39

Chapter 13 – Early Lessons: White Boys Groomed as Leaders, Black Boys Groomed as Athletes or Preachers - Introduction: Childhood as Destiny 41

Chapter 14 – The Untapped Power of the Whole Brain 43

Expanded Content

Chapter 1 Expansion – Plantation Faith & the Making of the Pulpit 46

Chapter 2 Expansion – The Preacher as the First "Office" for Black Men: A Platform When Few Existed 48

Chapter 3 Expansion – Money, Malachi, and Misreadings: The Sacred Text Meets the Ledger.. 49

Chapter 4 Expansion – Prosperity vs. Prophecy 51

Chapter 6 Expansion – Black Church vs. White Church 52

Chapter 8 Expansion – A Legacy of Resistance 53

Chapter 9 Expansion – The Global Stage 54

Chapter 10 Expansion – The Future of Black Leadership 55

Chapter 11 Expansion – A Call to Action 56

Chapter 12 Expansion – The Difference Between a White Man's Theology Training vs. a Black Man's Training 57

Chapter 13 Expansion – Early Lessons: White Boys Groomed as Leaders, Black Boys Groomed as Athletes or Preachers 58

Chapter 14 Expansion – The Untapped Power of the Whole Brain 59

Plantation Faith & the Making of the Pulpit

On American plantations, faith was inhaled like oxygen. In the worst conditions known to humankind, enslaved families gathered in hush arbors-secret meetings under trees, in fields, behind cabins-to sing, testify, and hold one another together. Faith was medicine, map, and memory. It told a people that Pharaohs fall, seas part, and captives go free.

Yet faith on the plantation was also surveilled and shaped. Slaveholders allowed or appointed "slave preachers" who emphasized obedience and heavenly reward over earthly justice. Passages about submission were spotlighted; Exodus and Jubilee were dimmed. The pulpit's message became the battlefield: Was the sermon a lullaby or a signal? Was it training people to wait-or teaching them to walk?

In this furnace, the Black preacher's role formed. He (later, sometimes she) was the only public voice with a platform. The preacher prayed at funerals, blessed marriages, mediated disputes, and interpreted God to a people fighting to stay human. He was more than clergy; he was counselor, teacher, and diplomat between the oppressed and those in power. After emancipation, the church became the first stable Black-governed institution: it bought land, founded schools, and organized mutual aid. The pulpit was our podium because few others existed.

But the arrangement carried a price. When survival depends on not provoking the lash-or later, the law-messages bend toward safety. In every era, some pulpits preached comfort where confrontation was needed. Others did the opposite, using scripture as a sword for civil rights, labor rights, and liberation. The pulpit has never been neutral. It is either an engine for movement or a museum for memory.

As migrations remapped Black America-from rural South to urban North, from West Side neighborhoods to southern suburbs-the pulpit retained pride of place. Politicians learned to court it. Reporters learned to quote it. When the nation wanted "the Black view," it called a pastor. That visibility brought influence, but it also narrowed the image of Black leadership to Sunday morning. Meanwhile, outside those walls, policy was being written, budgets passed, contracts awarded, and international alliances forged-often without us.

This is the tension the chapters ahead explore: How do we honor the

appropriations bill? The plantation built our pulpit. Now we must build our power.

Malcolm X

From "Message to the Grassroots" (1963): On unity across differences for real power. (Good primary transcripts and historical hosts available.)

Elijah Muhammad

"Christianity... is one of the most perfect Black-slave-making religions on our planet."

Louis Farrakhan

"There really can be no peace without justice. There can be no justice without truth. And there can be no truth, unless someone rises up to tell you the truth."

The Preacher as the First "Office" for Black Men:
A Platform When Few Existed

In the aftermath of Emancipation and through the long shadow of Jim Crow, Black communities needed institutions that could be built with the resources at hand: sweat equity, small donations, land pooled by congregants, and an unbreakable belief that tomorrow from today. The church answered that need. It offered a roof, a lectern, a ledger, and a schedule – Sunday and midweek, reliably. When other doors were closed, the sanctuary was open. When other titles were denied, the honorific "Reverend" could be earned, bestowed, and defended by the people.

Within that space, the preacher's role crystallized as a kind of first public office accessible to Black men. He mediated disputes, organized relief when a home burned down, read letters for those who couldn't, and negotiated with city officials who otherwise ignored the neighborhood. In a world rationing dignity, the pulpit conferred it.

This accessibility mattered. Professional pathways-law, medicine, elected politics, corporate management-were narrowed by statutes and custom. The pulpit, by contrast, required a vocation, a community's consent, and the discipline to serve. It demanded learning-scripture, history, rhetoric-even where formal schooling was scarce. It let a man test and hone leadership in the most intimate polity available: the congregation.

Vocation and Structure

The office of preacher is part calling, part craft, part institution. The calling supplies moral direction; the craft furnishes technique-voice control, textual interpretation, counseling; the institution provides continuity-bylaws, trustees, auxiliaries, a budget. When these three align, the church becomes more than a place of worship. It becomes a training ground for governance.

Many pastors learned to chair meetings with fairness, to set agendas, to manage budgets under constraint, to rally volunteers, to build consensus when emotions and doctrine ran hot. Those are statecraft skills in miniature. From a sociological view, the pulpit served as a civic classroom where leadership could be practiced weekly, observed publicly, and corrected communally.

Visibility is both opportunity and risk. As preachers became the most reachable spokespeople for Black neighborhoods, outside institutions-newspapers, universities, city hall, party machines-began to treat the pastor as the authorized voice of a people. That recognition could bring resources: a grant for the food pantry, a new stop sign near the school, a meeting with a hospital board about staffing. But it could also narrow the image of Black leadership to one genre-religious-and funnel political energy through persuasive speech rather than binding policy.

Thus the tension: the pulpit amplified the community's voice while sometimes inadvertently gatekeeping other voices-organizers, educators, entrepreneurs, policy analysts-whose work is equally essential to power. The result could be an overreliance on sermon as solution, as if eloquence alone could substitute for economic strategy or legislative design.

Economics and the Ethics of Provision

Every institution requires money. Roofs leak; lights burn; food pantries need food. The Black church from its earliest days was a miracle of small contributions-nickels and dollars assembled into schools, burial societies, choirs, and scholarships. In this context, the pastor's stewardship of funds became a moral crucible.

When stewardship is transparent-budgets published, priorities debated, outcomes measured-the offering plate is an instrument of mutual aid. It converts devotion into groceries, tuition, and rent relief. When stewardship turns opaque, guilt-driven, or performative, it can corrode trust and convert worship into transaction. The difference is not theological; it is administrative. The teachings of Jesus do not exempt a ledger from audit.

Debates around tithes illustrate this clearly. A text like Malachi 3 is not a blank check; it is a passage with context, history, and competing interpretations. One may argue for disciplined giving and still insist that churches practice the same fiscal accountability we demand of public offices. The preacher, as the church's chief fiduciary, must model the ethic expected from mayors and school boards: clarity about costs, candor about limits, and courage to reprioritize when need demands.

Formation: Rhetoric to Realism

The pulpit excels at formation-shaping imaginations with story, scripture, and song. People leave a strong service with courage to sit through zoning meetings; the fluency to translate moral claims into clauses enforceable by law. The preacher who treats Sunday as launchpad rather than destination-who moves members from pews into school board seats, union caucuses, neighborhood associations, procurement offices-turns spiritual capital into public capacity.

Some churches have long done this: training voter registrars, hosting credit unions, incubating small businesses in the basement fellowship hall, teaching homeowners about appraisals and appeals. Here, the preacher's office touches the city's machinery. The sermon's "go ye" becomes a calendar of committees.

The Politics That Courts the Pulpit

Because congregations can be mobilized, politicians court pastors. Courting is not in itself corrupt; advocacy should be pursued wherever people gather. But the courtship can distort incentives. Leaders become brokers - exchanging endorsements for promises that never appear in a budget line. Photo-ops substitute for policy. The danger is that proximity to power is mistaken for power itself.

The safeguard is institutional literacy: knowing how appropriations are made, where regulations are drafted, who writes the implementation memos, what data gets reported, and how to read it. A church that cultivates this literacy-and expects it of its shepherd-cannot be cheaply flattered. It measures outcomes, not handshakes.

The Gendered Story We Must Tell Honestly

Calling the pulpit the "first office for Black men" risks erasing women's leadership-mothers, organizers, teachers, deaconesses, evangelists, and pastors whose work held churches upright and communities together. Any honest account must name this: women funded, staffed, and strategized ministries while too often being barred from the very office they sustained. Correcting that record is part of maturing beyond a single leadership archetype. A future of shared power begins with accurate memory.

Beyond the Walls: From Symbol to System

The office of preacher has symbolic reach: robes, processions, sacred texts. Symbols matter; they bind stories to a people. Yet systems change lives: fair appraisals, enforceable labor standards, accessible credit, reliable transit, safe housing. The wisest pastors move easily between the two-blessing symbols that nourish identity while training

In practice this looks like:

Publishing annual financials and programming outcomes to the congregation.

Teaching members how school funding formulas work and how to influence them. Building partnerships with unions, clinics, universities, and small-business suppliers.

Training congregants to serve on commissions and boards where decisions get made.

Holding candidates' nights that focus on budgets, not slogans.

The Risks of Celebrity

Modern media can turn a pastor into a brand. Branding is not ministry; it is marketing. When sermon clips outrun service to the poor, when building campaigns eclipse investments in people, when applause replaces accountability, the "first office" degrades into a stage. The antidote is proximity to need and a governance culture that values the quiet competence of treasurers, clerks, and committee chairs as much as the charisma of the pulpit.

A Larger Horizon of Offices

If the preacher was the first accessible office, it must not be the last. The point is not to abandon pulpits but to multiply offices: council seats, planning boards, procurement desks, bank underwriting teams, accreditation boards, newsroom editorial tables, international NGOs, and diplomatic corps. Leadership diversified across these sites can do what no sermon alone can: stabilize households, reform rules, and secure futures.

Continuity Without Captivity

We honor our elders by building on their foundations without becoming captive to their forms. The early church housed schools because public systems would not. Today, where public systems exist, churches can become power partners-watchdogs and co-laborers ensuring those systems serve everyone. The preacher's office remains vital as conscience, convener, and coach; it is strengthened, not diminished, when joined by a chorus of other offices.

Money, Malachi, and Misreadings:
The Sacred Text Meets the Ledger

Every movement of people has required resources – land to meet on, food to share, tools to build with, books to learn from. The early Black church was no different. Out of the ashes of slavery and into the fragile promise of Reconstruction, communities pooled scarce funds to buy timber for a sanctuary, to print hymnals, to bury their dead with dignity. Dollars mattered because dollars carried dignity.

Into this context, scripture was not an abstract idea; it was a map of survival. Yet the way scripture was interpreted – especially passages about tithes and offerings – would shape not only worship but also wealth. Malachi 3:8 became one of the most frequently cited verses in Black pulpits across America:

"Will a man rob God? Yet ye have robbed me. But ye say, Wherein have we robbed thee? In tithes and offerings."

The verse carried an aura of thunder. For many congregants, it settled the question before it was asked: giving money was not optional but holy. To withhold it was to rob God Himself. But a closer reading, paired with historical context, shows that this verse referred not to cash offerings in modern churches but to agricultural support for temple maintenance in ancient Israel.

This is where the pulpit's authority and the ledger's reality collide. When interpretation narrows to guilt – "pay or you rob God" – giving is coerced rather than cultivated. When interpretation broadens to stewardship – "invest in God's house as you invest in your own household" – giving becomes a covenant rooted in clarity.

Anglo-Saxon Roots of the "Tithe"

Even outside scripture, the idea of the tithe has a complicated lineage. In Anglo-Saxon England, a tithing was an administrative unit of ten households, bound to one another by responsibility and law. It was not primarily religious but social, economic, and legal. From these early European practices, the idea of "tithing" as a set contribution entered English-speaking Christianity.

The Black church inherited not just biblical echoes but this Anglo-European framework – one that had long tied money, governance, and

are wielding centuries of economic expectations.

The Burden of the Plate

For many poor and working-class Black families, the offering plate has been both a blessing and a burden. On one hand, collective offerings built institutions no one else would fund: schools, credit unions, mutual aid societies, and HBCUs. On the other hand, the constant push to give – sometimes under threat of spiritual punishment – drained households already fighting to keep lights on.

Malcolm X saw this contradiction clearly:

"When you go to a church and you see the pastor... with a philosophy and a program that's designed to bring Black people together and elevate Black people, join that church!... But when you see a program designed to take from you without giving back, leave it."

Elijah Muhammad sharpened the critique:

"Christianity... made Blacks worship a false, White god... taught to turn the other cheek... wait until the next life for justice."

In this light, financial manipulation from the pulpit was not just about money; it was about delaying justice – promising heavenly reward while extracting earthly resources.

Transparency vs. Secrecy

Healthy churches post their budgets, explain their bills, and let members see where every dollar goes. Unhealthy churches veil their accounts behind spiritual authority. The difference is night and day: transparency breeds trust; secrecy breeds suspicion.

Louis Farrakhan warned:

"We must not shrink from the responsibility of pointing out wrong, so that we can be comfortable and keep White people comfortable in their alienation from God."

Replace "White people" here with "anyone in power who benefits from silence" and the principle remains. Silence around finances is complicity. Speaking truth about stewardship is not betrayal – it is fidelity to God and people alike.

Prosperity Gospel: The Modern Mutation

In the late 20th century, a new preaching trend took root – the so-

wealth, that tithes were not only obedience but also "seed money" for God's blessings. Preachers flying private jets and living in mansions were framed not as exploiters but as proof of God's favor.

For struggling families, the message was intoxicating: give more, believe harder, expect abundance. But this theology twisted the cross into a lottery ticket. Jesus fed thousands with loaves and fish; He did not build palaces with donations.

Nathan Hare critiqued this dynamic as part of a larger pattern:

"There is a White determination to regard Black people as 'White' without rewarding them and treating them as White or making them as educated or affluent."

Applied here: the prosperity gospel lets Black congregants perform wealth through giving without delivering structural wealth through ownership, education, or investment. It satisfies appearance but not reality.

Julia Hare and the Psychology of Giving

Julia Hare, the "female Malcolm X", often spoke about how psychology shapes Black family life. While not always addressing tithes directly, her insights reveal how deep-seated expectations of loyalty and sacrifice can be exploited. She taught that people give out more longing – longing for hope, belonging, affirmation. But when institutions exploit that longing, they turn devotion into dependency.

The psychology of giving, then, is not just economics; it is identity. To refuse to give may feel like refusing God, family, or community. To give, even when bills remain unpaid, may feel like choosing righteousness over selfishness. Preachers who manipulate this psychology are not simply mismanaging money – they are wounding the soul.

Alec Baldwin: An Outsider's Reminder

Even voices outside the Black church context, like Alec Baldwin, have noted America's tendency to remain uninformed about the deeper realities shaping lives. Speaking on political ignorance, Baldwin said:

"Americans are too often uninformed about the world around them."

Applied to our subject: too often congregations are uninformed about the economics of their own churches. They give but do not know. They sacrifice but do not see the receipts. This ignorance is not

From Obligation to Investment

The future requires a shift: from seeing offerings as obligation to seeing them as investment. Investments demand transparency, accountability, and return. A church that asks for 10% must show what that 10% accomplished – not in vague "spiritual blessings" but in concrete outcomes: youth programs, scholarships, food pantries, housing initiatives, legal aid.

This shift does not diminish faith; it dignifies it. It aligns spiritual generosity with tangible justice. It fulfills the biblical vision that "faith without works is dead."

Conclusion: Ledger as Mirror

Money reveals priorities. In a sense, the church budget is more honest than the church mission statement. Words can be lofty; numbers are blunt. They tell us whether we value buildings more than people, pastors more than congregants, spectacle more than service.

The misreading of Malachi 3:8 and the manipulation of offerings have too often made the pulpit a drain instead of a fountain. But reclaimed, the offering plate can be what it was in the hush arbors: a tool of survival, a vote of confidence, a collective act of resistance against poverty and neglect.

The question is not whether to give – but how giving is governed.

And in that governance lies the difference between robbery and resurrection.

Prosperity vs. Prophecy
Introduction: The Cross or the Cadillac?

When we ask what it means to be a spiritual leader, we are faced with a sharp contrast: a man walking dusty roads with nothing but his words and his courage, or a man stepping into a luxury car after delivering a sermon that raised half a million dollars. Both call themselves ministers of the gospel, but the distance between them could fill a canyon.

The ministry of Jesus was radical simplicity. He had no building fund, no media empire, no bank account. His work was people – the blind, the lame, the widowed, the orphaned, the outcast. He did not demand ten percent of their wages; He multiplied their loaves and fishes. His sermons were not about prosperity in this life or the next but about justice, mercy, forgiveness, and the in-breaking of God's kingdom.

Contrast this with the rise of the modern prosperity gospel, where wealth is preached as proof of divine favor and luxury is displayed as evidence of faith. Here, the preacher becomes not prophet but celebrity, not servant but brand.

The tension between prosperity and prophecy is not new. It is as old as the prophets of Israel who cried out against kings feasting while the poor starved. It is as current as pastors defending their private jets while congregants ride buses. The question is the same: will the pulpit be a voice for the powerless or a platform for the powerful?

Jesus the Prophet, Not the Celebrity

To understand how far we have drifted, we must look clearly at the record of Jesus. He was, by every account, a man of the margins. He lived without permanent home, borrowed boats, and was buried in a borrowed tomb. His followers were fishermen, tax collectors, zealots, and women of scandalous reputation. His miracles were not staged performances but intimate moments: spit and mud on blind eyes, bread broken in back alleys, demons cast out of forgotten children.

The authority of Jesus did not come from possessions but from presence. He entered villages not with fanfare but with focus. He spoke not in polished phrases designed to impress donors but in parables that unsettled the powerful. His ministry was prophetic because it was willing to risk everything – comfort, approval, even life itself – for the sake of

When the crowds gathered, He often slipped away. When the rich young ruler approached, He challenged him to give everything away. When Pilate offered Him a chance to save Himself, He refused. This was not prosperity; this was prophecy.

The Prosperity Preacher's Creed

Now consider the modern celebrity pastor. He speaks of "seed faith" and "harvest." He tells struggling families that if they give their last dollar, God will multiply it. He builds sanctuaries that look like stadiums, complete with jumbotrons and smoke machines. His sermons are broadcast worldwide, his face plastered on book covers. his brand carefully managed.

For him, prosperity is both theology and marketing. A jet is not excess but "efficiency." A mansion is not greed but "evidence." A luxury car is not vanity but "a testimony." Every possession becomes a sermon illustration, every indulgence reframed as divine reward.

And yet, behind the gloss, the math is cruel. Congregants give out of desperation, but their lives do not change. They are promised breakthrough but delivered bills. The preacher thrives on their hope but rarely shares their hardship.

Malcolm X: A Voice Against the Hustle

Malcolm X saw through this dynamic decades ago. He warned that many preachers were hustlers in holy clothing. He once said:

"The White man will try to satisfy us with symbolic victories rather than economic equity and real justice. He'll let us march all we want as long as we stay in church and out of power."

The prosperity gospel is the ultimate symbolic victory: sermons that feel like empowerment but never restructure power. The preacher becomes a showman, the congregation becomes an audience, and justice is postponed indefinitely.

Elijah Muhammad: The False Promise of the Hereafter

Elijah Muhammad echoed this critique, pointing to Christianity's emphasis on the next life as a form of control:

"Christianity... taught [Black people] to turn the other cheek... to wait until the next life for justice."

Prosperity preaching updates this strategy. Instead of waiting until

of heaven: a delay tactic to keep people compliant.

Louis Farrakhan: The Duty to Tell the Truth

Louis Farrakhan issued a stern warning to preachers:

"All of us who are leaders, all of us who are preachers, we must not shrink from the responsibility of pointing out wrong, so that we can be comfortable."

Prosperity preaching shrinks from this duty. It does not point out wrong – it points to dreams. It does not confront injustice – it comforts the comfortable. It trades the risk of prophecy for the safety of prosperity.

Nathan and Julia Hare: Psychology and Illusion

Nathan Hare, as a sociologist, reminds us that illusions of progress often pacify real demands for justice. If congregants believe wealth is a matter of faith, they may stop fighting for better wages, fair housing, or equal schools. The prosperity gospel turns structural injustice into individual failure.

Julia Hare would add that the psychology of self-worth is at stake. A believer who tithes faithfully but remains poor is left to blame himself – "I must not have enough faith." The system never takes the blame. The preacher never refunds the tithe. The guilt always falls on the giver.

Alec Baldwin: The American Distraction

Even Alec Baldwin's critique of American ignorance applies here. He once remarked that Americans are often uninformed about global realities. In the church, this ignorance becomes cultivated: congregants are kept uninformed about budgets, investments, and the preacher's salary. They are distracted by spectacle while the economics of their own congregation remain hidden.

The Prophetic Alternative

What would it look like if churches rejected prosperity and reclaimed prophecy? It would look like budgets opened for inspection. It would look like pastors living modestly, not extravagantly. It would look like offerings funding schools, health clinics, and legal aid instead of luxury cars.

It would look like Jesus – traveling light, preaching truth, feeding multitudes, standing with the marginalized, risking His life for justice.

empowers the people.

Conclusion: Choosing Our Model

The choice before the Black church is stark: will we follow the path of prosperity or prophecy? One promises quick blessing but delivers little. The other demands sacrifice but delivers freedom. One fills pews with promises of abundance; the other may empty pews but fills streets with change.

The preacher who embraces prophecy may never own a jet or a mansion. But he will own something far greater: the trust of his people and the witness of history. And perhaps, in God's eyes, that is the only prosperity that matters.

The Politics of Preaching
Introduction: From Sermon to Strategy

The pulpit has always been more than a place of worship. It is a platform of influence. In the Black community especially, the preacher's voice carries a weight that politicians, activists, and media moguls envy. It is no accident that every election cycle, candidates find their way into church pews. They know the pulpit is not only a spiritual stage but a political amplifier.

But the question is not whether politics touches the pulpit. The real question is: does the pulpit shape politics, or does politics shape the pulpit? When politicians court preachers, who benefits – the community or the candidate?

The Legacy of Political Pulpits

From the days of slavery, the pulpit was one of the only platforms a Black man could mount without permission from a White overseer.

Sermons became not just scripture lessons but coded political messages. Spirituals carried double meanings: "Steal Away" meant both prayer and escape. The preacher became both minister and messenger.

After emancipation, Black churches served as organizing centers. They hosted meetings for voter registration, literacy campaigns, civil rights rallies. The pulpit was not a spectator seat; it was a command post. Martin Luther King Jr. himself launched a global moral movement from church pulpits across the South. His sermons were political by necessity, because segregation was not only a sin but a statute.

This legacy shows the prophetic power of political preaching: when pulpits challenge unjust laws, they become engines of liberation.

When Politics Courts the Pulpit

But over time, the relationship became complicated. Politicians realized that rather than fight the pulpit, they could court it. Instead of silencing preachers, they could flatter them. A preacher with a large congregation could deliver votes. A preacher with a reputation could deliver legitimacy.

So candidates came with handshakes, promises, and photo opportunities. They offered recognition in exchange for endorsements.

Sometimes this benefited communities – when churches negotiated for resources, programs, or reforms. But too often, it became a one-way transaction: politicians gained votes while congregations gained little more than slogans.

The Illusion of Influence

To be courted feels like power. To be called upon by governors or presidents can feel like equality at last. But proximity is not power. A preacher can meet with presidents and still watch his people remain in poverty. He can sit at banquets while his congregants struggle to buy groceries.

Malcolm X warned against this illusion:

"The White man will try to satisfy us with symbolic victories rather than economic equity and real justice."

Being photographed with a senator is a symbolic victory. Securing jobs, healthcare, and housing for the people is real justice. The challenge is that too many preachers settle for the former while neglecting the latter.

Elijah Muhammad: Independence Before Endorsements

Elijah Muhammad offered an alternative model: independence. He taught that Black communities should build their own schools, businesses, and farms rather than depend on promises from politicians. He distrusted the courtship between pulpit and politics because he saw it as another form of control.

For Elijah, real power came from self-reliance – not from handshakes with political leaders but from ownership of institutions. His model was limited in scope but prophetic in principle: no people can negotiate from weakness.

Farrakhan: The Danger of Silence

Louis Farrakhan also cautioned leaders about compromising truth for comfort:

"We must not shrink from the responsibility of pointing out wrong, so that we can be comfortable."

When preachers cozy up to politicians, they risk shrinking from that responsibility. They may mute their sermons to avoid offending allies. They may bless candidates rather than challenge them. They may turn

The cost of that silence is high: communities remain uninformed, unorganized, and unempowered.

Nathan and Julia Hare: The Psychology of Political Dependence

Nathan Hare emphasized how systems condition Black communities to rely on external validation. When churches place too much faith in politicians, they teach dependence rather than independence. Julia Hare added that this shapes psychology: congregants learn to cheer for appearances instead of demanding outcomes.

When the preacher boasts of meeting with the mayor but cannot show new housing permits or improved schools, the congregation has been trained to mistake visibility for victory.

Alec Baldwin: The Wider Lens

Even Alec Baldwin's critique of American ignorance speaks here.

He pointed out that Americans are often uninformed about global realities. Similarly, congregations are often uninformed about political processes. They hear speeches but don't know how budgets are passed, how policies are implemented, or how lobbying works. This ignorance keeps them vulnerable.

The pulpit that truly empowers must teach political literacy: how to read a city budget, how to pressure school boards, how to organize voter blocs that demand policies, not platitudes.

Prophetic Politics vs. Pulpit Politics

There is a difference between prophetic politics and pulpit politics.

Prophetic politics: confronts leaders with truth, defends the marginalized, refuses to compromise core values for access.

Pulpit politics: trades endorsements for favors, prioritizes visibility over substance, and confuses access with authority.

One builds justice. The other builds illusions.

Conclusion: The Pulpit Must Decide

The pulpit cannot avoid politics, but it can decide what kind of politics it will practice. Will it be the politics of photo opportunities or the politics of prophecy? Will it trade truth for access, or will it use access to demand justice?

who walk out of that service empowered.

    The preacher who chooses prophecy over politics may lose invitations to banquets, but he will gain something far greater: a community that knows how to govern itself.

Black Church vs. White Church
Introduction: Two Sanctuaries, Two Stories

On Sunday morning, America is both most divided and most united. Divided, because Black and White Christians often worship in separate sanctuaries. United, because the rituals – hymns, prayers, sermons, offerings – follow similar patterns. But beneath the surface, the purposes and outcomes of these churches differ profoundly.

For centuries, Black churches have functioned as survival engines, while White churches have functioned as inheritance keepers. Black congregations built institutions to resist poverty and racism; White congregations maintained institutions to preserve privilege and power. Both call themselves churches, but they occupy very different roles in America's racial drama.

The Black Church: Survival and Sacrifice

The Black church was born in chains. On plantations, hush arbors became sacred spaces where enslaved people prayed for deliverance. After emancipation, church basements doubled as schools, meeting halls, and credit unions. In the Jim Crow era, churches organized protests, boycotts, and voter-registration drives.

The Black church's theology has always been survival theology.

Sermons comforted the weary, spirituals encoded escape plans, and tithes kept lights on in communities neglected by the state. Giving was sacrificial: families who had little gave anyway, trusting God to make a way.

The Black preacher emerged not only as a pastor but as counselor, teacher, activist, and negotiator. He filled roles denied to Black men elsewhere. The church became the first stage, the first bank, the first college, the first insurance company.

The White Church: Wealth and Inheritance

The White church followed a different path. Its roots lay in colonial power, land ownership, and established denominations. Sanctuaries were funded by wealthy patrons, pews reserved for prominent families, and seminaries endowed by old money.

Offerings were not given out of desperation but from surplus.

already had resources: universities, hospitals, publishing houses.

White churches did not need to serve as survival centers because their communities were already buffered by privilege. Instead, they functioned as inheritance keepers: preserving cultural dominance, reinforcing social networks, and sometimes justifying racial hierarchy with theology.

The Contrast in Worship and Wealth

Walk into a Black church, and you may find worship marked by passion, energy, and improvisation – a survival language, a way of wringing joy out of sorrow. Walk into a White suburban church, and you may find order, predictability, and wealth-coded aesthetics – polished choirs, expensive sound systems, well-funded youth programs.

This contrast is not about culture alone but about economics. A Black church may fund its programs with offerings from struggling families; a White church may fund its programs with endowments and investments. The difference in wealth accumulation translates into differences in influence.

Nathan Hare pointed to this disparity when he critiqued how systemic racism denied Black communities equal education and economic reward. The White church benefits from generations of accumulated privilege, while the Black church scrapes together resources in spite of systemic denial.

Theology of Forgiveness vs. Theology of Liberation

White churches often emphasized forgiveness, individual morality, and personal salvation. These teachings, while valuable, sometimes allowed congregants to ignore systemic injustice. A plantation owner could beat slaves during the week and sit in church on Sunday, convinced that personal repentance secured his salvation.

Black churches, by contrast, developed a theology of liberation. Exodus became the central narrative: God delivers captives. Jesus became not just savior of souls but liberator of the oppressed. Sermons carried political weight because survival itself was political.

Elijah Muhammad critiqued Christianity for making Black people worship a White God and wait for justice in heaven. His critique applied especially to White churches that sanctified oppression under the banner of faith.

Politicians understand these differences. When seeking forgiveness or stability, they turn to White churches. When seeking votes or moral legitimacy, they turn to Black churches. This duality reveals how America views religion; White churches as power brokers, Black churches as mobilizers.

Malcolm X warned that White institutions were content to let Black people sing and shout in church as long as they stayed out of power. The contrast between pulpits shows how this strategy works: White preachers could become senators and presidents; Black preachers were kept at pulpits, praised but politically sidelined.

Julia Hare: The Psychology of Dependency

Julia Hare observed that the church shaped not only worship but self-perception. For Black congregants, loyalty to the church became loyalty to community survival. But when the church failed to deliver material results, that loyalty could breed dependency rather than empowerment.

Meanwhile, White congregants often saw church as an accessory to lives already enriched. Their dependency was not survival but status.

This psychological difference explains why Black churches often overflowed with sacrificial giving while White churches quietly accumulated endowments.

Alec Baldwin: Ignorance and Illusion

Alec Baldwin's critique of American ignorance applies again here. Most White congregants remained uninformed – or willfully blind – to the suffering of Black communities. Their churches rarely taught them about systemic racism; instead, they taught them about personal morality. This ignorance allowed them to feel righteous while benefiting from oppression.

Toward Honest Comparison

To fault White congregations today for their inherited wealth is to misunderstand history, but to ignore that history is to misunderstand justice. The Bible itself acknowledges generational consequences: sins of fathers visit their children. Wealth and poverty, too, are generational.

The Black church must ask: will it continue to imitate White models of wealth and respectability, or will it lean into its prophetic legacy of liberation? The White church must ask: will it confess its complicity in

Conclusion: Two Choices, One Future

The contrast between Black and White churches is not absolute – there are prophetic White congregations and complacent Black congregations. But as patterns, the differences matter.

The Black church was born in survival, forged in fire, sustained by sacrifice.

The White church was born in privilege, protected by power, enriched by inheritance.

The future demands more than comparison. It demands collaboration. If the Black church brings its prophetic fire and the White church brings its accumulated resources, together they could build a new model of justice. But only if honesty precedes unity.

Power, Psychology, and Control
Introduction: The Battle for the Mind

Chains can be broken, laws can be repealed, and walls can be torn down. But the most difficult form of bondage to break is psychological. A people can be free on paper yet still enslaved in thought. They can walk without shackles yet live with the reflexes of captivity. Religion, at its best, renews the mind and frees the spirit. At its worst, it reinforces the very chains it claims to shatter.

This chapter explores how faith in the Black community has often been shaped – and sometimes twisted – into a system of control. We look at the generational trauma of slavery, the so-called Willie Lynch doctrine, and the ways in which sermons became both balm and bondage. At the center is the question: does the pulpit empower the people to govern themselves, or does it train them to submit to others?

The Willie Lynch Narrative

Though historians debate the authenticity of the Willie Lynch Letter, its ideas capture a chilling reality: divide and control. The letter allegedly instructed slave owners to sow division – young against old, light against dark, male against female – and to use fear and dependency to secure obedience for centuries.

Whether or not Lynch himself wrote such a letter, the strategy is undeniable. Enslaved families were terrorized into patterns of fear. Mothers pleaded with masters to spare their husbands, children learned to thank God for survival while fearing man for punishment. Over generations, this dynamic produced a psychology of survival that often confused submission with piety.

Fear, Faith, and the Family

Consider the scene: a master raises his whip. A wife begs, "Please, in the name of God, spare my husband." The husband is humiliated but alive. The children witness everything. They learn that survival comes not from resistance but from pleading, praying, and complying.

This script was replayed daily. Over time, fear of the master fused with reverence for God. The line blurred: to disobey the master felt like disobeying God; to thank God was to thank the system for sparing your life. This is how control seeps no only into laws but into souls.

Slaveholders understood the pulpit's power. They allowed select enslaved men to preach – but only sermons that emphasized obedience. "Servants, obey your masters." "Turn the other cheek." "Great is your reward in heaven." These verses, repeated weekly, conditioned minds to equate holiness with docility.

Elijah Muhammad was blunt:

"Christianity... is one of the most perfect Black-slave-making religions on our planet."

His words sting, but they capture the reality: religion was weaponized as restraint. It pacified rebellion by redirecting anger into worship, promising future reward instead of present justice.

Malcolm X: Unity of Purpose vs. Control

Malcolm X cut to the heart of the matter:

"We do not condemn the preachers as an individual but we condemn what they teach. We urge that the preachers teach the truth... unity of purpose."

For Malcolm, the preacher was not the enemy. The true enemy was the manipulation of messages that kept people divided, blind, and dependent. A pulpit preaching unity was a weapon of liberation. A pulpit preaching obedience without justice was an instrument of control.

Nathan Hare: The Psychology of Internalized Oppression

Nathan Hare, the first architect of Black Studies, understood that slavery's chains had left scars on the psyche. He argued that internalized oppression taught Black people to see themselves through the eyes of the oppressor. This meant constantly questioning their worth, distrusting their own institutions, and deferring to White authority.

In the church, this often meant that congregants elevated the preacher as the one authorized voice – even above their own collective agency. Instead of developing many leaders, churches trained people to follow one man, mirroring the plantation hierarchy.

Julia Hare: The Gendered Dimension

Julia Hare highlighted how these dynamics also shaped gender roles. Women, who had often been the backbone of survival – raising children, working, giving – were frequently silenced in pulpits. Their labor was celebrated but their leadership denied.

female, elevate one while suppressing the other. Churches that barred women from leadership perpetuated control rather than liberation. Correcting this imbalance is not just about inclusion; it is about breaking psychological chains that teach half the community to follow and never lead.

Louis Farrakhan: Truth as Disruption

Louis Farrakhan insisted that leaders must not shrink from speaking uncomfortable truths:

"There can be no justice without truth. And there can be no truth unless someone rises up to tell you the truth."

Control thrives in silence. When preachers avoid truth – about racism, economics, politics – they leave congregants in a fog. When they dare to speak truth, they disrupt control. A sermon can either rock a cradle or shake a system.

Alec Baldwin: Ignorance as a National Disease

Even Alec Baldwin's critique of American ignorance speaks here. A nation uninformed about global affairs is easily manipulated by propaganda. A congregation uninformed about its own history, psychology, and power is equally vulnerable. Ignorance is not simply absence of knowledge – it is a strategy of control.

When churches fail to teach history, economics, and political literacy, they are not neutral. They are complicit in keeping people docile.

Toward Empowered Minds

If control is maintained by ignorance and fear, liberation requires knowledge and courage. This means:

Teaching history beyond slavery – Africa before chains, resistance during bondage, victories after emancipation.

Explaining economics – how banks, credit, and debt work; how to organize cooperatives and businesses.

Training leaders – not just one preacher, but many congregants in skills of negotiation, advocacy, and governance.

Challenging gender hierarchies – elevating women to leadership as equals.

Such teaching transforms the pulpit from a platform of control into a

Conclusion: Breaking the Script

The psychology of control is powerful because it is scripted and repeated. But scripts can be rewritten. A new script says: God is not a master's ally but a liberator's friend. Leadership is not confined to one man in a pulpit but shared by a community of trained, courageous people. Faith is not a lullaby for submission but a trumpet for action.

The pulpit must decide whether it will reinforce the old script or write a new one. The difference is not abstract; it is generational. Minds freed today raise children who think differently tomorrow. And that is how control is broken – not just once, but forever.

A Legacy of RESISTANCE
Introduction: Prophets or Puppets?

The Black preacher has always stood at a crossroads. On one side lies the temptation to pacify, to preach comfort and obedience, to keep pews full and masters (or modern power structures) satisfied. On the other side lies the call to prophecy: to tell truth, to risk reprisal, to lead people not only to heaven but toward justice on earth.

The history of the Black church is filled with both kinds of preachers. Some became puppets, repeating the language of control. Others became prophets, shaking nations. This chapter traces the legacy of resistance – the preachers who chose prophecy over prosperity, truth over silence, and liberation over comfort.

Nat Turner: The Fire in the Pulpit

In 1831, Nat Turner, an enslaved preacher in Virginia, led one of the most significant slave rebellions in American history. Turner believed he was divinely inspired to break the chains of slavery. His sermons were not soothing lullabies but coded calls to action. He preached Exodus not as metaphor but as mandate.

Turner's rebellion terrified the South and inspired the enslaved. His legacy reminds us that the pulpit has always had revolutionary potential. To preach can mean to pacify – or to incite. Turner chose resistance, and his name endures because he refused to make the pulpit a cage.

Absalom Jones and Richard Allen: Building Independent Institutions

Not all resistance was violent. In the late 1700s, Absalom Jones and Richard Allen, both formerly enslaved, resisted discrimination within White Methodist churches. When forced to pray in segregated balconies, they walked out and founded independent Black congregations. Allen went on to establish the African Methodist Episcopal (AME) Church, the first independent Black denomination in America.

Their resistance was institutional. They showed that independence was possible, that Black churches could govern themselves, own property, and lead without White oversight. Their legacy lives in every Black denomination that exists today.

Preaching was not the domain of men alone. Sojourner Truth, born enslaved in New York, became a fiery preacher and abolitionist. She used her voice to denounce slavery and sexism alike, declaring, "Ain't I a woman?" Her sermons were prophetic because they confronted both racial and gender hierarchies.

Her legacy challenges churches that silenced women in pulpits.

Resistance includes breaking gender chains as well as racial ones. Sojourner's life proves that prophetic voices cannot be contained by tradition.

Martin Luther King Jr.: The Dream as Demand

Martin Luther King Jr. embodied the prophetic pulpit in the 20th century. His sermons were soaked in scripture but aimed at systems. From Montgomery to Memphis, King used the church as headquarters for civil rights, his words echoing far beyond sanctuary walls.

King's dream was not sentimental but strategic. It demanded integration, economic justice, and an end to war. He was jailed, threatened, and ultimately assassinated. His legacy reminds us that prophetic preaching carries a cost – but it also moves mountains.

Malcolm X: The Revolutionary Voice Outside the Pulpit

Though not a traditional preacher, Malcolm X's voice functioned with prophetic intensity. He critiqued the church for pacifying Black people, yet he preached in his own way: speeches that sounded like sermons, laced with scripture, history, and searing critique.

Malcolm showed that prophecy does not require a pulpit. Any platform where truth is spoken boldly becomes sacred ground. His resistance was intellectual, rhetorical, and political, reminding us that the prophetic voice can rise inside or outside the church.

Louis Farrakhan: Truth-Telling in the Modern Age

Louis Farrakhan carried this prophetic mantle into contemporary times, challenging preachers to tell the truth even when uncomfortable: "There can be no justice without truth. And there can be no truth unless someone rises up to tell you the truth."

Farrakhan's leadership has been controversial, but his insistence on truth as the foundation of justice is prophetic. He stands in the tradition of preachers who refused silence, regardless of consequences.

For every Nat Turner, there were preachers who urged slaves to obey. For every King, there were pastors who warned their congregations not to march. For every Sojourner Truth, there were men who silenced women. This double legacy forces us to ask: what kind of preacher will history remember?

The prophetic preacher is remembered for courage; the complicit preacher is forgotten or condemned. The choice is always present: puppet or prophet.

Nathan and Julia Hare: Prophets Beyond the Pulpit

Resistance is not only the task of preachers. Nathan Hare, in founding Black Studies, created an academic pulpit where history and psychology were taught as tools of liberation. Julia Hare, with her fiery speeches, functioned as a preacher without a church, calling Black families to psychological and spiritual independence.

Their work proves that prophecy is broader than sermons. It is any truth-telling that frees minds and builds institutions.

Conclusion: Choosing the Prophetic Path

The legacy of resistance shows us that the pulpit can be a throne of control or a trumpet of liberation. Nat Turner, Sojourner Truth, Richard Allen, Martin Luther King Jr., Malcolm X, Louis Farrakhan, Julia Hare, Nathan Hare – each in their way chose prophecy over silence.

Their lives remind us that to resist is not optional but essential. To preach without resistance is to betray the gospel itself.

The question for today's preachers is the same as for those who came before: Will you be a puppet who pacifies, or a prophet who resists?

The Global Stage
Introduction: From Pulpit to Presidency

If the pulpit is the highest office many Black men have traditionally held, the presidency has been the highest office for White men. This contrast is not accidental; it is structural. White men have historically pursued and secured global leadership – running empires, commanding militaries, presiding over nations. Black men, shut out of those spaces, often turned inward, leading congregations but rarely countries.

This chapter explores how leadership ambitions were shaped by history, law, and culture. We ask why White men sought world leadership while Black men were directed to pulpits, and how this imbalance continues to shape power today.

Empire as Ambition

From Europe's colonial ventures to America's global dominance, White men pursued leadership not just nationally but internationally. They sailed oceans, conquered lands, and established governments. Their theology – particularly in Protestant traditions – often supported this ambition. The "city on a hill" became justification for empire.

The pulpit for them was not the final destination but a stepping stone. Ministers often became politicians, educators, or businessmen. In White communities, religion served power rather than replacing it. The church was an institution among many, not the only platform available.

The Black Church as Substitute Throne

For Black men, denied political office and economic mobility, the pulpit became the substitute throne. Here, they could command respect, exercise authority, and lead people. But the scope was limited. A congregation may have numbered hundreds or thousands, but it was not a nation. The preacher could bless marriages and funerals, but he could not pass laws.

Malcolm X: Symbolic vs. Real Power

Malcolm X warned of symbolic victories:

"The White man will try to satisfy us with symbolic victories rather than economic equity and real justice."

The Black preacher's pulpit was often a symbolic throne. It looked

symbolic rather than structural. Real power writes budgets, signs treaties, commands armies. Symbolic power fills pews but cannot change laws.

Elijah Muhammad: Building Nations, Not Just Churches

Elijah Muhammad understood this distinction. He rejected the church as the ceiling of Black leadership. Instead, he preached nation-building: schools, businesses, farms, and banks. His vision was flawed in execution but correct in scope. He taught that true power meant building institutions that could rival those of the dominant society, not just preaching sermons within walls.

His legacy challenges us: Are we satisfied with pulpits, or will we build nations?

Louis Farrakhan: Global Consciousness

Louis Farrakhan expanded this perspective by positioning Black people within global struggles. He reminded his followers that they were part of a worldwide community – Africa, the Caribbean, the Middle East. He insisted that leadership required global consciousness, not just local sermons.

"We, the Black people of America, were chosen by Allah... to carry a message to the whole of humanity."

For Farrakhan, the pulpit was not enough. The stage was the world.

Nathan Hare: Structural Exclusion

Nathan Hare analyzed how systemic racism restricted Black men's access to global leadership. Even when qualified, they were funneled into symbolic roles rather than strategic ones. This structural exclusion meant that many of the most brilliant leaders of the Black community were confined to pulpits, classrooms, or community organizations rather than national and international power.

Julia Hare: Psychology of Limitation

Julia Hare pointed to the psychological impact of these limits. When generations of young Black men saw preachers as the highest form of leadership, they internalized that ceiling. Ambition was redirected from political office to pastoral office, from international negotiations to Sunday sermons. The psychology of limitation became self-perpetuating.

Even Alec Baldwin's critique of America's ignorance has relevance here. America, as a nation, has often been parochial – focused inward, uninterested in global awareness. This narrowness reinforces the imbalance: White elites still dominate global politics, while Black leadership is often confined to domestic moral issues.

The Obama Exception

Barack Obama's election in 2008 was hailed as a breakthrough – a Black man ascending not just a pulpit but the presidency. Yet his rise was framed as exceptional, a one-time event rather than a new normal. The fact that his election was celebrated as historic proves how rare such global leadership roles remain for Black men.

Conclusion: From Symbol to System

The global stage demands more than sermons; it demands strategies. White men sought empires; Black men were too often confined to pulpits. But history is not destiny. The task of this generation is to move from symbolic leadership to systemic leadership – from pulpits to parliaments, from sermons to strategies, from churches to chambers of power.

The question remains: Will we remain content with pulpits, or will we claim presidencies?

The Future of Black Leadership
Introduction: Beyond the Walls

Every generation faces the same question: where will its leaders come from? For Black America, the answer for centuries has been the pulpit. From Nat Turner to Martin Luther King Jr., the preacher has been the face of leadership. But in the 21st century, new spaces have opened: politics, business, technology, entertainment, activism. The pulpit is no longer the only stage.

This chapter explores the future of Black leadership – where it is emerging, how it differs from the past, and what it must avoid to truly liberate our people.

A New Generation Leaving the Church

Across America, younger generations are leaving organized religion in large numbers. Surveys show that millennials and Gen Z are less likely to attend church regularly, less likely to tithe, and more skeptical of institutional authority. For the Black community, this shift is profound.

Where once every young man dreamed of being a preacher, now many dream of being entrepreneurs, activists, or influencers. Social media has replaced the pulpit for some. Hashtags mobilize marches. Podcasts teach political literacy. Instagram lives function as modern sermons.

This is not the death of faith but the redirection of energy. Leadership is migrating beyond the sanctuary into digital, economic, and political spaces.

Politics as a New Pulpit

For generations, politicians visited churches to secure votes. Today, more young Black leaders are becoming the politicians themselves. From city councils to Congress, mayors to governors, Black political leadership is expanding. This is crucial: policy, not sermons, determines school funding, healthcare, housing, and policing.

The future preacher must either become politically literate or step aside for leaders who are. The ballot is as sacred as the Bible. The budget is as decisive as the benediction.

Economic power has always undergirded freedom. Enslaved Africans were exploited for labor; freed Africans were denied land, credit, and capital. Today, Black entrepreneurs are reclaiming economic agency. From tech startups to real estate ventures, from restaurants to investment firms, Black business leaders are reshaping the future.

Nathan Hare argued that economic dependency was a form of bondage. The future must prove him right – by building ownership, not just employment. Leadership will belong not just to those who can preach but to those who can provide jobs, housing, and wealth.

Women at the Forefront

The future cannot look like the past if it silences half the community. Women have always been the backbone of the Black church – funding, organizing, sustaining – yet often barred from pulpits. Today, Black women are leading movements, corporations, political campaigns, and churches.

Julia Hare warned against gendered dependency and championed women's leadership. The future must elevate women as equal leaders, not helpers. A community that sidelines its women cripples itself. A community that empowers its women doubles its strength.

Global Consciousness

Louis Farrakhan reminded us that Black people in America are part of a global struggle. The future of leadership must be global. Africa, the Caribbean, Latin America – all face similar battles against neocolonialism, poverty, and systemic racism.

Future leaders must think beyond neighborhoods and even beyond nations. They must negotiate trade, climate policy, and global justice. The Black leader of tomorrow must be as comfortable in the U.N. as in the pulpit.

Media and Culture as Platforms

Malcolm X once said the media is the most powerful entity on earth because it controls the minds of the masses. Today, media platforms are pulpits. Black filmmakers, musicians, and writers shape narratives as profoundly as preachers once did.

The future of leadership includes cultural architects who awaken minds through film, music, and literature. This too is prophecy, though delivered in images and lyrics instead of sermons.

Alec Baldwin's critique of American ignorance remains instructive. He noted how uninformed Americans are about global realities. Black leadership must not repeat this mistake. The next generation must be globally literate – understanding trade, technology, and international politics. Without that awareness, even the most passionate sermons will be provincial.

Balancing Faith and Function

This is not a call to abandon the pulpit. Faith still matters. Spirituality still fuels resistance. But faith must function. The preacher of the future cannot simply preach prosperity; he must preach policy, economics, and empowerment. He must partner with activists, educators, and entrepreneurs.

The pulpit must become not a throne but a hub – one node among many in a network of leadership.

Conclusion: The Next Chapter of Leadership

The preacher was the first office. The future must multiply offices. Black men and women must lead in government, in boardrooms, in schools, in media, in international institutions. The pulpit must not be the ceiling of our ambition but the foundation of our expansion.

The question is no longer why do Black men become preachers while White men seek world leadership? The question is: will Black men and women now seek world leadership themselves?

The future will not be written in sermons alone. It will be written in laws, investments, art, and global alliances. The pulpit lit the fire. Now the world must feel its heat.

A Call to Action
Introduction: From Question to Charge

This book began with a question: Why do Black men become preachers while White men seek world leadership? We have traced the history, the psychology, the economics, and the politics that shaped that reality. We have seen how the pulpit became the first office for Black men, how offerings and tithes shaped survival, how prosperity preaching distorted truth, how politicians courted pastors, how Black and White churches diverged, and how prophetic voices resisted control.

Now we must move from history to strategy, from question to charge. The time for observation is over. The time for action is now.

Step One: Redefine Leadership

Leadership must no longer be confined to pulpits. Preachers remain important, but they cannot be the only leaders. We need leaders in city halls, in corporate boardrooms, in schools, in hospitals, in technology firms, in unions, and in international agencies.

The pulpit should be a training ground, not a throne. It should prepare men and women to lead beyond its walls. Every sermon should end with an invitation not just to the altar but to the world.

Step Two: Demand Transparency

Offerings are not robbery if they are investments. Churches must open their books, publish their budgets, and prove their impact. If a congregation gives faithfully, it deserves receipts. Transparency builds trust. Secrecy breeds suspicion.

Imagine if every church produced an annual report: number of scholarships given, families housed, meals served, laws influenced. This would restore the offering plate as a tool of liberation, not exploitation.

Step Three: Build Economic Power

Economic independence is the bedrock of freedom. We must move beyond giving to sustaining. This means creating credit unions, cooperatives, and community investment funds. It means buying land, building businesses, and teaching financial literacy.

Nathan Hare warned of economic dependency; the antidote is ownership. Faith without works is dead, and faith without economic

Step Four: Embrace Women's Leadership

The future of Black leadership cannot repeat the mistakes of the past. Women have always been the backbone; now they must be the forefront.

Julia Hare reminded us that silencing women cripples communities. Empowering them doubles strength. Churches must ordain women, movements must elevate women, and families must teach daughters that their voices are as prophetic as any man's.

Step Five: Think Globally

Louis Farrakhan insisted that our struggle is global. We must see ourselves as part of a worldwide movement for justice. This requires learning international politics, building alliances across Africa and the diaspora, and ensuring our voices are present in global forums.

Alec Baldwin's critique of American ignorance applies here: ignorance limits power. Global literacy expands it.

Step Six: Speak Truth, Always

Malcolm X called for unity of purpose. Elijah Muhammad warned against waiting for justice in heaven. Farrakhan demanded that leaders tell the truth even when uncomfortable. The thread connecting them all is courage.

Preachers and leaders must stop shrinking from truth. They must speak about racism, poverty, sexism, corruption, and injustice. Silence is complicity. Truth is liberation.

The Role of the Pulpit Going Forward

The pulpit must remain, but its purpose must change. It must no longer be a throne of control but a hub of empowerment. Sermons must inspire not just feelings but plans. Congregations must leave not only with hope but with strategies.

The pulpit must train leaders for every sector – teachers, lawyers, entrepreneurs, activists, diplomats. It must bless not only weddings and funerals but also business launches and political campaigns.

Conclusion: From Sermon to System

The journey of this book has shown that the pulpit has power but limited scope. White men historically sought world leadership because their systems allowed it. Black men historically became preachers

But the future is not fixed. We can choose differently. We can honor the pulpit without being confined by it. We can preach and we can legislate, we can worship and we can own, we can sing and we can strategize.

The call to action is simple yet profound: move from sermon to system, from pulpit to policy, from prayer to power.

The question that began this journey must now become a challenge: Will we remain content with pulpits, or will we seek presidencies? Will we settle for symbolic victories, or will we demand structural change?

The answer is not in the preacher's mouth alone. It is in the people's hands.

The Difference Between a White Man's Theology Training vs. a Black Man's Training
Introduction: Same Scriptures, Different Schools

On paper, theology should be universal. It studies God, scripture, morality, and the human condition. But in practice, theology is shaped by context. White men and Black men may open the same Bible, but the institutions, expectations, and outcomes of their training are vastly different. One is trained for power; the other often for survival.

White Seminaries: Gateways to Power

For centuries, White men studied theology in seminaries attached to prestigious universities. Princeton, Harvard, Yale – many of these began as theological institutions. Their students were not just taught scripture; they were taught governance, philosophy, languages, and leadership.

Theology training for White men was a passport to influence. Graduates often became pastors of wealthy congregations, presidents of universities, chaplains to politicians, and eventually political leaders themselves. Theology was not merely spiritual – it was institutional and civic.

Black Seminaries: Training for Containment

Black men, by contrast, were often excluded from White seminaries. When allowed, they were relegated to segregated programs or denied leadership roles. Historically Black seminaries like Howard School of Religion, ITC in Atlanta, or Payne Theological Seminary arose out of necessity, not invitation.

Their mission was noble: to train Black ministers for Black congregations. But the scope was often limited. Instead of preparing men to run universities, lead nations, or shape global policy, Black seminaries focused on preparing men to preach and pastor within the constraints of Black neighborhoods.

Theology here was survival-based, not system-based. It emphasized care for the flock, endurance under oppression, and salvation in the afterlife. Rarely did it train men to see themselves as governors, judges, or presidents.

White seminaries: philosophy, law, governance, classics, Hebrew, Greek, policy engagement.

Black seminaries: homiletics, pastoral care, church administration, scripture memorization, evangelism.

Both important, but one prepared men to lead nations; the other prepared men to sustain neighborhoods.

Elijah Muhammad and Malcolm X: A Critique of Training

Elijah Muhammad argued that this difference was deliberate – that White men's theology was designed to empower, while Black men's theology was designed to pacify. Malcolm X echoed this critique, insisting that most Black preachers were trained to keep their people docile rather than mobilized.

Their critiques ring true: training is never neutral. Who funds the institution, who writes the curriculum, and who certifies the degree all determine what kind of leader emerges.

Conclusion: Rewriting the Curriculum

For the future, Black theology must expand. It must not only train pastors to preach but also thinkers to govern, scholars to write policy, and leaders to engage global challenges. Theology should not be a cage but a launching pad.

The difference in training is not inevitable. It is a choice. And it is time to choose differently.

Early Lessons: White Boys Groomed as Leaders, Black Boys Groomed as Athletes or Preachers
Introduction: Childhood as Destiny

Leadership does not begin in college or seminary; it begins in childhood. What a boy is told he can be shapes what he believes he should be. In America, the lessons diverge sharply by race.

White boys are taught early to be leaders of nations and industries.

Black boys are too often funneled into narrow lanes: athletics or preaching. This is not coincidence – it is conditioning.

White Boys: Groomed for Governance

From the earliest grades, White boys in affluent communities are encouraged to lead. They are placed in debate clubs, student governments, and leadership camps. Parents groom them to inherit businesses, run for office, and take command.

They grow up seeing presidents, CEOs, judges, and governors who look like them. The expectation of leadership becomes normal.

Leadership is not a dream; it is destiny.

Black Boys: Funneled to Courts, Fields, and Pulpits

By contrast, Black boys are often steered into athletics or church.

Teachers tell them they can be basketball stars, football players, or preachers. Rarely do they hear, "You could be a senator," or, "You could run a Fortune 500 company."

The imagery reinforces it: posters of athletes on walls, sermons praising preachers as heroes, but little exposure to Black men leading corporations or writing laws. The choices narrow: either entertain or inspire. Both are important, but both are limiting if they are the only options.

Malcolm X: The Illusion of Opportunity

Malcolm X saw this pattern clearly:

"The White man will try to satisfy us with symbolic victories rather than economic equity and real justice."

Athletics and preaching can become symbolic victories – celebrated,

public policy. Both are contained within boundaries set by others.

Julia and Nathan Hare: The Psychology of Expectation

Julia Hare warned about how expectations shape self-image. If Black boys are constantly told they can only succeed with a ball or a Bible, they internalize those limits. Nathan Hare added that this is part of structural racism – funneling talent away from law, medicine, and governance into entertainment or religion.

The result is predictable: generations of boys grow up dreaming of being the next Le Bron James or the next T.D. Jakes, while few dream of being the next Barack Obama or the next Thurgood Marshall.

White Boys Groomed for the World, Black Boys Groomed for the Block

The difference is stark:

White boys inherit networks, mentorship, and expectation of leadership.

Black boys inherit sermons, sports, and survival strategies.

This gap explains why White men dominate global leadership positions while Black men dominate pulpits and sports arenas. Both visible, both celebrated – but vastly unequal in structural power.

Conclusion: Teaching New Lessons

The future depends on changing what we teach our children. Black boys must hear from their earliest days that they can be world leaders, governors, innovators, and thinkers. They must see models of Black men and women in these roles.

Athletics and preaching are not to be abandoned – they remain vital. But they must no longer be the ceiling. They must be part of a wider spectrum of options.

The message must shift: You can be more than a player or a preacher. You can be a policymaker, a president, a world leader.

The Untapped Power of the Whole Brain

For centuries, education in America has been shaped not simply by curriculum, but by a system of expectations that differs sharply between Black children and White children. One of the least examined, but most damaging realities of this system, is the failure to train Black children to fully use the left and right sides of their brains.

From the earliest years of life, White children are taught to think broadly, to analyze critically, and to apply creativity toward leadership. Their education often integrates the arts and sciences, blending logic with imagination, mathematics with music, history with vision. The result is a type of balanced cognitive training that develops both hemispheres of the brain. This is not accidental-it is deliberate. A White child is groomed to see himself not just as a participant in the world, but as a potential leader of nations.

By contrast, the Black child's education has historically been shaped by limitation. Too often, he is pushed into narrow lanes of expression: entertainment, sports, and the pulpit. While White children are trained to govern, Black children are trained to perform. One group is taught to master the world, the other to please it.

Nathan Hare, in his groundbreaking work on Black psychology, noted that the conditioning of Black youth is rarely about unlocking the full spectrum of human potential. Instead, it is about containment. Schools in Black communities are underfunded, arts programs are cut, and critical thinking is underdeveloped. Creativity is often stifled unless it leads to entertainment. Logical, analytical thought is rarely tied to visions of leadership. The brain, therefore, is not trained holistically; one hemisphere is starved while the other is overstimulated.

Julia Hare spoke passionately about this imbalance, reminding us that the education of Black children has long been shaped by forces that want compliance rather than independence. When the left brain is trained without the right, the result is mechanical thought without vision. When the right brain is stimulated without the left, the result is creativity without discipline. True leadership requires both.

Louis Farrakhan has echoed this idea in his own way, urging Black people to stop depending on others to define their destiny. He argues that without reclaiming both logic and imagination-without fusing reason with faith, creativity with discipline-Black leadership will always remain

Consider the contrast: A White boy may be sent to debate clubs, chess tournaments, and music lessons-each one stimulating a different part of his brain. By the time he is a man, he has learned to reason, to plan, to dream, to persuade, and to create. A Black boy, on the other hand, is often pushed toward basketball, football, or performance arts. He may develop skill and confidence, but his education of the whole brain is incomplete. His training is not for ruling nations, but for entertaining them.

Malcolm X warned of this psychological trap. He said: "The White man will try to satisfy us with symbolic victories rather than economic equity and real justice." These symbolic victories include the Black superstar athlete, the celebrated preacher, or the admired entertainer. They represent recognition, but not real power. They reflect a society that rewards Black excellence only when it entertains or pacifies, never when it threatens to govern.

The untapped power of the whole brain, then, is not merely a neurological issue – it is a systemic one. For Black people to move from pulpits and playing fields to boardrooms and world stages, three must be a revolution in education. Parents must demand schools that nurture both sides of the brain. Communities must encourage children to pursue math and science as vigorously as they pursue music and athletics. Leaders must model a balance of discipline and imagination.

Elijah Muhammad once taught that knowledge of self is the beginning of power. Knowledge of self includes not only knowing who we are historically, but knowing what our minds are capable of. The Creator did not design the Black mind to be limited to halftime shows and Sunday sermons. He designed it to build civilizations, to direct nations, to transform humanity.

The challenge before us is to unlock the full capacity of our children. If we continue to allow one hemisphere of the brain to remain dormant, we will continue to produce generations that are brilliant in flashes but powerless in the halls of leadership. If we begin to educate both hemispheres equally, then the Black child can become not just a preacher or an athlete, but a statesman, a scientist, a philosopher, and a world leader.

The destiny of a people is hidden in the training of their children. When we begin to train the whole brain of the Black child, we will begin to see the whole power of the Black race.

Whole-brain education is not a slogan; it is a design. It trains analysis and imagination together, marries discipline to wonder, and turns knowledge into service. In this frame, the mind is not a container to be filled but a craft to be honed.

"Be transformed by the renewing of your mind." – Romans 12:2

The Four Pillars

Logic (Left-brain discipline): numeracy, argument, coding, evidence, research design.

Imagination (Right-brain vision): music, visual art, design, poetry, theater.

Embodiment (Habits that last): time-blocking, note systems, memory techniques, public speaking, team sport as leadership lab.

Ethics (Why it matters): service learning, civic literacy, scripture and moral philosophy in conversation with real dilemmas.

"Education is the passport to the future, for tomorrow belongs to those who prepare for it today." – Malcolm X

A Church-Home-School Compact

Church: host a mid-week "Whole-Brain Lab" (math circles+ music theory; debate+ drama).

Home: create a 45-minute evening rhythm (15 learn, 15 make, 15 move) with a quiet corner for focused work.

School/After-School: pair AP/IB or honors courses with arts electives and maker projects; require one civic project per term.

"There can be no justice without truth." – Louis Farrakhan

Chapter 1 Expansion
Plantation Faith & the Making of the Pulpit

The greatest danger is not oppression.

It is adaptation.

People adapt to cages. They decorate them.
They defend them.

They even fear leaving them.

When the pulpit became the only respected office for Black men, ambition did not die – it was redirected. Young men did not stop dreaming. They just learned to dream smaller.

Not because they lacked intelligence. Not because they lacked courage.

But because the world showed them where they were allowed to stand. Dreams are shaped by visibility.

If you never see a Black man signing treaties, you will not dream of diplomacy. If you never see a Black man running banks, you will not dream of finance.

If you never see a Black man writing laws, you will not dream of legislation.

But if you see a Black man every Sunday commanding a pulpit, you will dream of preaching. That is not spiritual destiny – that is social design.

The church did not cause this – but it absorbed it. And what it absorbed, it preserved.

That is why this book does not blame the pulpit.

It interrogates the system that made the pulpit necessary.

Chapter 1 is not about tearing down the church.: It is about understanding how survival can quietly become limitation.

The office trained voices – not architects. It trained performers – not planners.

That is not because preachers were evil.

It is because their office was designed for care, not control.

You cannot expect a nurse to perform surgery without training. You cannot expect a preacher to run governments without access.

But when no other office is visible, people begin to expect miracles from roles that were never designed to produce them.

So when the preacher could not stop poverty, people said, "Pray harder." When the preacher could not stop violence, people said, "Have more faith." When the preacher could not change policy, people said, "Wait on God."

Faith became a substitute for strategy. Waiting became a substitute for organizing. Hope became a substitute for power.

And substitutes always fail eventually.

The Preacher as the First "Office" for Black Men:
A Platform When Few Existed

The danger is not that the pulpit became important. The danger is that it became exclusive.

When leadership is locked inside one institution, creativity dies. People stop imagining new forms of power. They stop training for new kinds of leadership. They stop dreaming beyond what they see.

This is why some Black communities produce many pastors but few mayors. Many evangelists but few engineers. Many choir directors but few CEOs.

Not because talent is missing – but because vision is managed.

If leadership is always introduced through scripture but never through systems, people will believe that holiness matters more than competence. That emotion matters more than planning. That prayer matters more than policy.

But history shows something different:

Moses prayed – but he also confronted Pharaoh. Joseph believed – but he also ran Egypt's economy. Daniel worshiped – but he also advised kings.

Faith never replaced leadership. It fueled it.

The preacher was never meant to be the ceiling. He was meant to be the seed.

The tragedy is not that the pulpit rose – it's that nothing else rose with it.

The Bible never taught secrecy as holiness. It taught stewardship as responsibility.

If people give their last, they deserve to know its path.

Money, Malachi, and Misreadings:
The Sacred Text Meets the Ledger

Part 1

Giving is not just financial – it is emotional. People give because they want to belong. They give because they want to be seen as faithful. They give because they fear punishment. They give because they hope for miracles.

That makes the pulpit powerful – and dangerous.

A preacher can motivate generosity – or manipulate desperation.

When people are told: "Give and God will bless you," but never shown how God used the gift, faith becomes gambling.

People begin to give like they play the lottery – hoping for miracles instead of demanding structure. This creates cycles:

People give. They wait.

Nothing changes.

They blame themselves. They give more.

The system is never blamed. Only the believer.

That is not faith – that is emotional debt. True stewardship looks like

Money builds people, not just buildings. Money funds futures, not just floors.

Money trains leaders, not just singers. Money changes conditions, not just moods.

A church budget is a moral document. It shows what is truly valued.

If most money goes to buildings, the building is the god. If most money goes to leaders, leadership is the idol.

If most money goes to people, then God is honored.

Part 2

The future of giving must change.

People should not just give – they should own. Not just donate –

People are told:

"Give and God will multiply." But not taught: "Learn, build, organize, own."

So they give hoping for magic – while others build with math.

Prosperity vs. Prophecy

Part 1

Celebrity ministry changes the meaning of leadership.

When a preacher becomes a brand, people become consumers.

When a sermon becomes entertainment, truth becomes optional.

Lights, smoke, cameras, and screens can stir emotions – but they cannot build communities. A celebrity preacher must protect his image.

A prophetic preacher must protect his people.

That is the difference. Prophets offend. Celebrities please.

Prophets confront power. Celebrities court power. Prophets risk their lives. Celebrities protect their lifestyle.

Jesus was never trying to be famous. He was trying to be faithful. Fame came as a result – not a goal.

When pastors chase popularity, they lose prophecy. When they chase comfort, they lose courage.

Part 2

The prophetic preacher does not promise wealth. He demands justice.

He does not sell dreams. He organizes people.

He does not hide budgets. He opens books.

He does not live above his people. He lives with them.

This kind of preacher may never own a jet. But he will own trust.

Hospitals when hospitals rejected us. Courts when courts were unjust.

White churches did not have to become survival centers – because society already served them. This difference shaped theology.

Black theology cried, "God will deliver us."

White theology often whispered, "God has already blessed us." One prayed for freedom. The other prayed for stability.

Black Church vs. White Church

Part 1

In Black churches, money is emotional because it is scarce. In White churches, money is quiet because it is inherited.

Black families often tithe from struggle. White families often tithe from surplus.

That difference shapes power.

When you give from struggle, you give with hope. When you give from surplus, you give with control.

White churches often invest money. Black churches often survive on it.

This is not because of laziness. It is because of history.

Generations of stolen land, blocked loans, and denied opportunity created this gap. Worship reflects economics.

Part 2

White churches historically taught forgiveness without justice. Black churches taught survival through faith.

One protected power.

The other protected people.

But now the future demands something new: Faith plus justice. Worship plus strategy.

Prayer plus policy.

Black churches must not only survive – they must govern. White churches must not only inherit – they must repair.

Both must meet at truth. Learn. Build. Lead.

Faith must stop being a shelter from the world and become a tool to change it. Power begins in the mind.

Freedom begins in knowledge. Leadership begins in courage.

Part 1

The pulpit has always had two voices: One comforts power. The other confronts it.

Some preachers told people to wait. Others told people to rise. History remembers the risers. Nat Turner preached rebellion. Sojourner Truth preached equality.

King preached justice. Malcolm preached self-respect.

Their sermons were not safe – they were necessary.

Part 2

Prophets do not live long, comfortable lives. They are jailed.

They are threatened. They are killed.

But their words outlive their enemies.

Silence is safe – but it leaves people in chains. Truth is dangerous – but it breaks them.

Every generation must choose:

Comfort or courage. Silence or truth. Safety or freedom.

Part 3

Every preacher, leader, and believer must decide:

Will I protect my comfort – or my people?

Will I preserve tradition – or produce freedom?

The pulpit will always be powerful.

The question is:

Who will it serve?

The Global Stage

Part 1

Power is not local.

Power is global. Nations compete. Corporations dominate.

Resources move across oceans.

White men were trained to think globally. Black men were trained to think locally.

Not because of ability – but because of access. White leaders were taught:

How to negotiate treaties. How to control trade. How to build empires.

Black leaders were taught:

How to pastor neighborhoods. How to survive injustice. How to manage suffering.

One group learned to rule the world. The other learned to endure it. That was not destiny.

That was design.

Part 2

The pulpit looks powerful.

But real power signs laws. The pulpit sounds powerful.

But real power controls budgets. The pulpit feels powerful.

But real power moves armies, money, and markets.

Symbolic power comforts people. Structural power controls conditions.

Black leadership has often been symbolic – visible but limited. White leadership has often been structural – quiet but commanding.

The goal is not to abandon symbolism. The goal is to gain structure.

The Future of Black Leadership

Part 1

The future must look different. Black boys must see:

Presidents who look like them. CEOs who look like them. Diplomats who look like them. Scientists who look like them. Leadership must be reimagined. Not just holy – but strategic. Not just emotional – but institutional.

Not just local – but global. The pulpit lit the fire.

The world must now feel the heat.

Part 2

Leadership is changing. It no longer lives only in pulpits.

It now lives online, in businesses, in movements, and in politics. Young people do not wait for permission. They build platforms. Podcasts preach. Social media organizes. Hashtags mobilize.

The pulpit is no longer the only microphone.

Part 3

The future leader must know:

Politics. Business. Technology. Media. Global affairs.

Faith must walk with knowledge.

Prayer must walk with planning. Spirituality must walk with strategy.

Part 4

The preacher was the first office. Now there must be: Second offices.

Third offices. Fourth offices.

Leadership everywhere. City halls. Boardrooms. Classrooms. Courts. Global councils.

The future is not replacing the pulpit – it is expanding beyond it.

Chapter 11 Expansion
A Call to Action

Part 1

History only changes when people move. Not when they wait. Not when they hope.

Not when they fear. Action is faith in motion.

Part 2

Power must be built, not begged for.

Build schools. Build businesses. Build banks.

Build coalitions. Prayer opens doors.

Work walks through them.

Part 3

Truth produces change.

Leaders must speak – even when it costs. Faith that fears truth is not faith. It is fear.

The Difference Between a
White Man's Theology Training vs. a Black Man's Training

Part 1

Training shapes destiny.: White men were trained to govern. Black men were trained to pastor.

Not because of calling – but because of control. Education determines ambition.

Part 2

Policy. Economics. Law. Global affairs.

Faith must produce governors – not just pastors.

Early Lessons: White Boys Groomed as Leaders, Black Boys Groomed as Athletes or Preachers

Part 1

Children are taught before they choose. White boys are taught: You can rule.

Black boys are taught:

You can perform. This must change.

Part 2

Black children must hear:

You can lead nations. You can write laws. You can shape history.

Dreams are seeds.

What you plant is what you grow.

Part 1

Leadership requires the whole mind. Logic and imagination.

Strategy and vision. Math and creativity.

One-sided minds cannot lead whole nations.

Part 2

Education must prepare children not to survive – but to rule.

Art and science. History and futurism.

Faith and function.

The future belongs to thinkers, not just believers.

www.ingramcontent.com/pod-product-compliance
Lightning Source LLC
Chambersburg PA
CBHW060708030426
42337CB00017B/2798